THE XXL CRYSTAL HEALING BOOK FOR BEGINNERS

THE LIFE CHANGING SELF HELP GUIDE -
CHANGE AND ENHANCE YOUR LIFE WITH
THE POWER OF CRYSTALS

KAREN FREEMAN

Copyright © [2021] [Karen Freeman]

All rights reserved.

The author of this book owns the exclusive right to its content. Any commercial usage or reproduction requires the clear consent of the author.

ISBN – 9798495232464

Table of Contents

Introduction 1

    Attract Abundance into Your Life 2

Chapter 1: What is Crystal Healing? 4

    How Does Crystal Healing Work? 6

    The History of Crystals and Healing 7

    The Benefits of Crystal Healing 8

Chapter 2: Different Crystals And Their Uses 11

    Rose Quartz 12

    Quartz 13

    Obsidian 13

    Jasper 14

    Turquoise 15

    Citrine 16

    Amethyst 16

    Tiger's Eye 18

    Agate 18

Sapphire 19

Moonstone 20

Ruby 20

Bloodstone 21

Pyrite 22

Black Tourmaline 22

Chapter 3: How to Find The Right Crystal For You 25

Choosing The Best Crystal For Your Needs 27

Step 1 - Sit Down and Identify the Problem 28

Step 2 - Tune into Your Intuition 29

Step 3 - Look at Some Crystals 31

How to Look After Your Crystals 33

Chapter 4: Chakras and Crystal Use 36

What is a Chakra? 37

The 7 Chakras and What They Mean 38

The Root Chakra 39

The Sacral Chakra 40

The Solar Plexus Chakra 41

The Heart Chakra 42

The Throat Chakra 44

The Third Eye Chakra 45

The Crown Chakra 46

How do Crystals Help The Chakras? 47

Chapter 4: Getting Started With Crystal Healing 49

Programming Your Crystal 51

Simply Holding Your Crystal 55

Meditation With Your Crystal 57

Grounding Yourself 60

Crystal Exploration Meditation 62

Listening to Messages From Your Crystal 65

Getting What You Want Meditation 68

Balancing And Unblocking Chakras with Crystals 71

Addressing a Particular Chakra With Crystals 72

Using a Full Body Grid 75

Creating a Crystal Grid 78

Be Mindful of Your Intention 79

Identify The Right Crystals 80

Identify The Grid Pattern 80

- Lay Down Your Crystals 81
- Activate Your Crystal Grid 82
- Using a Crystal Altar For Manifestation 83
- Crystals And Yoga 85
- Place Crystals Upon Your Yoga Mat 86
- Place Crystals on Your Body 87
- Using Crystals in Your Daily Life 89
- Home And Work Space Placement 93

Conclusion 97

Disclaimer 102

INTRODUCTION

For many years, there has been a certain mystique around the use of crystals.

These beautiful natural stones look the part when displayed around the house, but did you know that they could also help to make you happier, healthier, more balanced, and could even attract more wealth and love into your life?

All from a shiny crystal!

Crystal healing falls under the spirituality and alternative medicine spectrum, which means there is a huge amount of interest and also skepticism attached to it. The truth is that crystals have been used in healing for centuries and even today, many people search for the right crystal to bring them the results they desire.

You've picked up this book because crystals interest you. Perhaps you're keen to learn more simply for interest's sake, or maybe you're interested in correcting a problem in your life. Whatever the reason, crystal healing is a wonderful addition to your life. You'll learn how to use these beautiful crystals to improve your health and wellbeing, whilst also decorating your home!

Attract Abundance into Your Life

In order for crystals to work, you need to believe in them. By cleansing negative energy and encouraging the flow of good energy, the crystals and their vibrations attract abundance, health, love, and wealth. Of course, which one comes your way depends on the type of crystal you choose; all crystals are known for different their different uses.

Throughout this book, you will learn everything you need to know to get started with crystal healing. From how to use crystals to the ones which are best for you, we'll teach you the basics to help pique your interest more. All you need to do is absorb the knowledge like a sponge and believe in the crystals and their innate power.

So, what is it that you want to attract into your life? Identify it now and then bear it in mind as you learn about the healing power of crystals. You can then refer back to our crystal guide whenever you have a different problem or use.

Open your mind, believe in the crystals, and allow them to do good work on your behalf.

Chapter 1:

What is Crystal Healing?

Before we can delve into how to use crystals and which crystal is best for you, we need to give you a thorough overview of crystal healing as a whole.

What is crystal healing? How can it help you? Does it have any scientific proof behind it? And where did it come from?

We're going to answer all of these questions before we get into the nitty-gritty of crystal healing.

So, let's define it.

Crystal healing is a form of alternative medicine but also has its roots in spirituality. For centuries natural crystals originating from the earth have been used to alleviate physical health symptoms and emotional problems. As the world's interest in spirituality grew, crystals were also used to manifest abundance, be it wealth, love, confidence, or something else entirely.

The great thing about crystal healing is that you don't need to have a deep background in spirituality. This is a form of healing and manifestation that is available to anyone. All you need to do is choose the right crystal and know what to do with it. By meditating on the crystal, carrying it with you at all times, and placing it in the right spot in your home, the crystals do their natural work.

How Does Crystal Healing Work?

The way in which crystals work is shrouded in mystery. For that reason, scientists are skeptical as to whether there is any solid basis to back up crystal healing and its claims. However, centuries of positive stories cannot be ignored!

As with most alternative therapies, the success of crystal healing comes down to belief in its ability to work. If you don't believe in it, it's not going to do much for you. The mind is a powerful thing.

Crystals are natural stones, and they emit vibrations that are undetectable to the human ear and eye. These vibrations, when harnessed and used in the right way can be used to unblock problematic body chakras, therefore allowing the free flow of good energy throughout the body. As a result, positive energy is in control, and the person concerned notices a marked improvement in the area of their life affected by that formerly blocked chakra.

Of course, chakras are energy centres within the body. There are 7 main chakras, and each is responsible for a specific part of your life or body. When that chakra becomes blocked or sluggish in its flow of energy, problems run amok. Crystals are used to release that blockage and encourage positive energy instead.

This can be done through meditation, but it can also simply be a case of carrying a crystal with you on a regular basis. We're going to talk in a lot more detail later in the book about how to use crystals and the particular type of crystal you need.

The History of Crystals and Healing

Crystal healing goes back centuries. Its first mention was from Plato when talking about Atlantis. Apparently, crystals were used to allow Atlanteans to read minds, yet the very first mention of the use of crystals in regular history dates back to the Sumerians, in 4500BC.

At this time, crystals were used firmly for spiritual means, and crystals were often broken down and used in spells and medicinal mixtures. It was around this time that the different methods of use for each specific crystal started to take shape. If something happened, i.e., someone was sick with a certain ailment, the specific crystal would be brought out and used in a tonic or healing ceremony, to counteract the problem. Crystals were also worn in jewellery, to ward off negative energy.

Crystals were also used during Ancient Egyptian times, Ancient Greece, and also in Ancient Rome. The use of crystals in India is also widely documented. Whether for use in jewellery or spiritual reasons, crystals have a long and decorated history.

The Benefits of Crystal Healing

The great thing about crystal healing is that it can be used for a huge range of different issues. Of course, it's not only for healing physical and emotional problems but also to help attract abundance. A few of the most common ailments treated with crystal therapy include:

- Anxiety
- Depression
- Insomnia and general sleeping problems
- Digestive problems
- Stress relief
- Negative thoughts and/or nightmares
- Confidence and self-esteem problems
- Low energy
- Emotional disturbances due to stress, relationship problems, etc

Of course, crystals are also used to help increase the amount of good energy in someone's life which, when used with the right intention and a belief in its ability to work, can help to attract love, health, and wealth.

Understanding crystal health is without a doubt best done in practice. Once you start to use crystals and start to see the benefits coming your way, you'll feel more confident to go further. At first, you might be sceptical, and that's fine. Sometimes it's normal to need a little proof that something is beneficial before your interest really grows. However, if you're completely sceptical, you need to open your mind and try it before you judge.

Crystal healing will only work when you believe it's going to. You have to approach healing with the right intention, e.g., with positivity and hope. That will give you the very best foundation on which to build.

So, now you know the basics of crystal healing, i.e., what it is, where it came from, and what it can do for you, let's delve into the crystals themselves.

Chapter 2:

Different Crystals And Their Uses

Each crystal has a specific use. That's why it's best to know what issue you want to address before you choose your crystal. Then, you'll have the very best chance of success.

In this chapter, we're going to talk about the most common crystals you'll find and their specific uses. To date, there are more than 200 different crystals, yet you're probably only ever going to use a handful. For that reason, we won't talk about all of them, only the ones that, as a beginner, will bring you positive results.

You'll also hear crystals referred to as gemstones, but they're one and the same thing. You can purchase crystals very easily these days. You can head online and find a huge range, or you can go to a new age store. It's best to go to a physical store if you can, as the people who work there are usually very knowledgeable and will help you to choose the stone that suits your needs best.

However, background knowledge will help you get started.

Rose Quartz

This is probably the most common crystal you will find and the one that you'll hear the most about. Rose quartz is a beautiful pink crystal that links to love - both the romantic kind and self-love too. If you're having problems in your relationship, rose quartz might help to bring about change and harmony in your union. This is also a crystal that is often used in times of heartache and grief, helping to soothe turbulent emotions.

Quartz

You'll also find clear quartz, which isn't translucent in colour and is actually white. This is an all-rounder crystal and is, therefore, a great choice for beginners. If you're struggling with concentration or even memory problems, clear quartz may help to bring about an improvement. This is also a good stone if you're lacking in energy, and you find that you're catching every bug and virus that is going around. Boosting your immune system is another of its benefits.

Obsidian

Obsidian is a beautiful black stone that derives from volcanic lava. This is a fantastic crystal for anyone who is feeling extremely negative or down and needs a little spiritual protection. For those who are struggling with identity and feels blocked in any way, meditation with obsidian may help to release blockages in specific chakras and help positive energy to flow.

Obsidian is associated with strength and clarity, so if you need to make an important decision, obsidian may help to give you the clear mindedness you need. It's also great for digestive issues and general detox.

Jasper

The stunning orange/red shade of jasper makes it a clear choice for decorative purposes, but it's also very beneficial for health and wellbeing. If you're struggling with stress, jasper should be your go-to stone. It helps to protect you from negative energy and helps to soak up negative energy that may be around you. As a result, confidence is increased, and clarity is achieved. Again, if you need to make a decision, jasper could be a good option.

Turquoise

As the name suggests, turquoise is a beautiful blue stone, which again, makes it a great option for jewellery. In crystal healing, turquoise is used to help bring balance to the three elements of your being - mind, body, and soul. It's also considered to be a pretty good stone for amplifying luck and can help to restore balance to emotions that may be a little turbulent at any particular time.

From a physical point of view, turquoise is great for respiratory issues, boosting a low immune system, and any musculoskeletal problems.

Citrine

Citrine is a very popular crystal and its beautiful amber colour really makes it pop in jewellery once more. This is a great stone if you want to boost your confidence levels and bring a boost of positivity to your life. If you're a negative thinker by default, citrine may help to relieve that negative energy and open the door for fresh, positive energy to enter. This is also said to be a great stone for those who are fearful of something, as it helps to bring clarity of thoughts.

If you're struggling with motivation and concentration, citrine may also give you the kick you need to get things done!

Amethyst

Everyone knows what amethyst looks like; it's one of the most common crystals around and again, it's a favourite in the jewellery world too. This is a stone that is extremely easy to incorporate into your daily life as you could simply wear a genuine amethyst bracelet on a day-to-day basis and grab the benefits.

From a crystal healing point of view, amethyst is purifying and protective. It's a good stone for those who are feeling down and negative, as it helps to ward off negative thoughts and energy. It's also a great stone for those who want to delve into their spirituality a little more, as the colour purple is the colour of the third-eye chakra, connected with wisdom. If you're struggling with sleep, amethyst could also help you to have a better night's sleep and also make some sense of any confusing dreams you're having.

From a physical point of view, amethyst s good for stress, pain conditions, and also for righting any hormone imbalances that may be causing problems.

Tiger's Eye

This stone is a truly beautiful one in appearance, with a brown and almost orange mixture to it. Of course, it's called the 'tiger's eye' because that's what it's supposed to represent! The golden hue of this stone makes it a popular option for decoration, but it has a wealth of uses.

If you're struggling with confidence, self-doubt, and you simply don't trust yourself to make the right choices, especially in your career, this crystal should be your go-to.

Agate

This beautiful blue/green crystal is a fantastic option for beginners. It helps to bring harmony to your mind, body, and should together and helps to get positive energy moving throughout your chakras. Negativity is also banished with the use of agate, while also boosting confidence, concentration, and memory.

If you have a project at work and you really need to focus and analyse data, use agate on a daily basis and notice the benefits. Your perception will be increased, and you'll be able to delve into data in a more detailed and concentrated way.

Sapphire

We all know that sapphire is a stunning stone that is often used in all different types of jewellery but it's also commonly used in crystal therapy. Not the cheapest stone, however, it's worth investing in if you seek wisdom in all things. Those who want to attract abundance and happiness into their lives should look towards sapphire and it's also a good option for boosting intuition too.

From a physical point of view, sapphire is thought to help with blood problems, stress, insomnia, anxiety, depression, and also helps with any eye problems you may have.

Moonstone

Moonstone is as popular for its name as it is for its beauty and benefits! Moonstone is a silver/white stone with smooth edges. It is a good crystal for beginners once more as it covers some basic and all-rounder benefits.

Moonstone is great for helping with inner strength and working towards growth. If you're starting over with something new, perhaps a new relationship or new job, moonstone will help you. It can help to reduce feelings of anxiety or worry connected to new beginnings and helps you to feel more positive about the future. If you want to enhance good luck, moonstone is another good choice.

Ruby

Ruby is another very common stone that is used in all types of jewellery but it's used in crystal healing too. If you're lacking in energy and you need a boost of positivity, ruby is the go-to option. It's known to help bring energy back into a lacking situation, but it's also known to help with mental tiredness too.

If you're struggling with libido, ruby is also connected to sex and general sensuality. The red colour is obviously fiery and sexy, which explains its general use! However, ruby can also be used for someone who is struggling with decisions and self-awareness.

From a physical point of view, ruby is good for detoxifying the blood and boosting circulation.

Bloodstone

Bloodstone has been used regularly throughout history to ward off negative energies but it can also help to detoxify your immediate environment. As with ruby, bloodstone is a good crystal for boosting circulation and detoxifying the blood.

Bloodstone can help with creative thinking, so if you have a project coming up, this could be a good crystal for you. It's also good for helping those who constantly think back to the past or worry obsessively about the future, helping you stay in the here and now. If you're regularly impatient or irritable, again, bloodstone is a good option.

Pyrite

When you set eyes on pyrite, you'll understand why so many people adore it! It's a stunning golden, sparkling crystal that can easily be worn as jewellery in conjunction with healing intentions. From a healing point of view, pyrite is often used to attract abundance in the form of money, and it can also boost concentration at work.

Black Tourmaline

As the name suggests, black tourmaline is a black crystal that looks a little like coal. However, it is ideal for anyone who is struggling with negativity and who wants to ward off negative energy. A proactive stone, black tourmaline is a good option for empaths as it can help to protect from negative vibes being emitted from other people.

Many people use black tourmaline close to their door, to help keep negativity out of the home, but it can be used almost anywhere, e.g., cars, workplaces, etc.

These 15 crystals are some of the most common you will find and they're also the ideal choices for a beginner in crystal healing. However, do remember that there are over 200 different crystals in existence and probably more appearing all the time! As more and more people enjoy the benefits of crystal healing, more research is being done and more crystals are being identified for their uses.

It's a good idea to keep an eye on new developments, just in case a different crystal pops up that may be ideal for your specific uses.

These crystals will be readily available online or in new-age stores. You won't struggle to find them, and you may like to build up a collection of different crystals so you can grab the one you need at any specific time.

You can use your crystals as decoration in your home, e.g., a large crystal ornament, a lamp, or simply small crystals left on a saucer. However, most people use crystals in jewellery or in prayer bead form. The choice of how you carry them is up to you, but in our next chapter, we're going to talk about how you can find the right crystal for your needs. Does the crystal choose you, or do you choose it?

Chapter 3:

How to Find The Right Crystal For You

Now you know about the different types of crystals on offer, you might be feeling a little overwhelmed as to which one to choose. Many crystals suitable for beginners have all-rounder properties and some overlap.

For that reason, you need to make sure that you really take your time when choosing the perfect crystal for your needs.

Now, that's not to say that if you randomly choose a crystal, it's not going to do anything for you. For sure, it will. However, it's best to choose a crystal that suits your needs and which you feel fully drawn towards before even attempting your first foray into crystal healing.

The right crystal will bring you the very best benefits. Then, as you start to notice advantages coming your way, you'll feel more encouraged to continue exploring crystals and their healing properties. Remember, there is a lot of scepticism around crystal healing, and you need to give yourself the best chance at really believing in the power of these natural stones. The best way to do that is to choose one that calls out to you. Then, you'll see that there is no space for scepticism, and only space for enjoyment and benefits.

In this chapter, we're going to talk about how to choose the right crystal. Then, we're going to explore how you can look after your crystal and make sure that its vibrations and energies remain in tip-top condition.

Choosing The Best Crystal For Your Needs

As you go through life, you'll find that you need different crystals for different situations. Sometimes you may be feeling a little anxious, other times you may be feeling jealous, and perhaps you start to feel lacking in confidence. Life is a cycle and our moods and needs change according to what we're encountering in our day-to-day existence.

So, when you choose a crystal, don't expect it to be the only one you ever need. You may choose one, great some great benefit from it, but then find that it doesn't suit another particular problem you're experiencing. In that case, you'll need to search for another crystal, better suited to that particular situation.

The good news is that there's a crystal out there for whatever you're dealing with.

Step 1 - Sit Down and Identify the Problem

What is it that you're feeling or lacking? Or, perhaps it's that you want something and you can't find a way to get it without needing an extra boost of something that you can't quite put your finger on.

You can't start to make use of crystal healing most effectively until you know what it is that you want or what you're looking for. A good way to identify these things, especially if you're struggling or feeling overwhelmed, is to sit down and write a journal.

Set aside half an hour every day to write your journal. You don't have to go into too much detail; keywords may be enough to help you identify the feelings you're grappling with and the things that your mind desires.

Continue journaling for up to two weeks, or until you start to see a pattern emerging. Once you do, that is likely to be the thing that you need a crystal to help you with.

By journaling and looking deep within, you're not being distracted by anyone around you. The point of crystal healing is that it's personal. Nobody can tell you what to do or what crystal you have to use. They can advise you, for sure, but they can't make you use a crystal that simply doesn't fit for you. New age store staff may be a good option if you're really struggling, but first, you need to identify the issue that's causing you the most annoyance or even distress and go from there.

Your intention for using crystal healing has to come from within.

Step 2 - Tune into Your Intuition

Once you know what your issue is, it's time to start finding the actual stone you're going to use to manifest change in your life. The best way to do this is to tune into your inner voice or your intuition. You'll no doubt have heard this called your gut feeling.

If you're not someone who tends to use their intuition much, you really ought to start. Trusting yourself is key to a happy and fulfilling life. When you rely upon your intuition to guide you, you're allowing higher forces to direct you in the direction you need to follow. This is also extremely useful when using crystals and messages and opportunities may crop up subconsciously and it's up to you to decide which route to take.

You'll no doubt have walked into a room before and felt something in your gut. It was either a good feeling or a bad one. That's your intuition trying to guide you towards or away from something. When you're trying to make a decision, your intuition is also a very powerful tool to help.

As the second step towards choosing the right crystal for your needs, simply start becoming aware of your intuition and what it's trying to tell you. Try this:

- Sit calmly and close your eyes
- Focus on your breath - Breathe in through your nose for a slow count of five, hold for a count of two, and then exhale through your mouth for a slow count of five. Repeat until you feel your mind calming
- Turn your attention to anything you're feeling. Do you have a feeling of dread? A feeling of curiosity?

What is it that you can feel bubbling under the surface?

- Tune into it fully and try and explore it a little. Do you notice any changes? Are there any images or words popping into your head?

Stick with this exercise for at least ten minutes a day and see if you notice any changes. You should find that you become automatically more aware of your inner voice/gut feeling/intuition in your daily life, simply because you're allowing it to flow and becoming more open to listening.

Step 3 - Look at Some Crystals

Now you need to take yourself to a place where you can look at crystals. If you're going to purchase them online, you should look at the webpage instead. In the last step we talked about tuning into your intuition, and that is going to help you here.

Look closely at the crystals on the page or in front of you. Do you feel a pull towards any in particular? It might feel like your attention is being dragged in one direction more than another. If so, try and pinpoint it down a little more and zone in on the particular crystal. In that case, the crystal has chosen you!

It might not be quite so obvious at first. It could be that a crystal catches your eye or that the name sticks in your head. No matter what you do, you can't quite forget about the look of it or its name. Again, that's the crystal trying to grab your attention.

Of course, you can simply do your research on which crystals are good for specific uses and then try and narrow your search down that way too. However, when you go down that route, still try and use your intuition to help pull you towards The One. Even if you look at crystals for manifesting love, for example, you'll find around three or four at least. Place them in a row or look at them on a screen and see which one your subconscious is pulling you towards.

At all times, when finding the right crystal for your needs, your subconscious will guide you. You simply need to be open to listening. The biggest mistake that most beginners in crystal healing make is just reading about crystals, finding one that fits the bill on a description, and then going for it. You need to put a bit more effort into it than that if you really want crystal healing to work for you.

How to Look After Your Crystals

Once you've gone to great lengths to choose your perfect crystal, you need to know how to look after it properly. As you use your crystal, it needs to be cleansed and kept in a safe place. Remember, crystals absorb negative energies and those energies can build upside the crystal if you don't look after it accordingly.

First things first, you need to show your crystal the utmost respect. This is a natural stone that has been around far, far longer than you or I! If you want your crystal to work hard for you, show it some respect. Don't leave it in the sun, don't throw it around, and always be sure to handle it with care and attention.

When you return home with your crystal or when it arrives at your home, you need to cleanse it. There are many people who have touched the crystal before you, and if you want it to zone in on your needs and desires, it needs to be completely cleansed and focused on what you want it to do. The residual energies of others are not going to help it do that.

To cleanse your crystal, simply follow these instructions:

- Rinse the crystal under running water, but make sure that it's not very hot and not freezing cold either - tepid water is perfect
- The water source needs to be natural, so if you can get to a stream, that would be the best option. If not, running water from a tap will suffice, or bottled water from a mountain stream. This will help to cleanse the crystal of any negativity that has attached itself to the stone

- To take things a step further, add a small amount of sea salt to the water
- You can also burn sage as you're cleaning the crystal, to eliminate negativity
- Leave your crystal out to dry in the light from a full moon if you can, or the morning sunshine, when it's not too hot
- Cleanse your crystal regularly, every week or two, to rid it of any built-up negativity

When storing your crystals, make sure that you keep them out of direct sunlight and away from extreme temperatures. A small box is perfect or even better, a cloth pouch. Keep your crystals close to your bed, either under your pillow or in a drawer next to where you sleep.

Of course, it's important to keep your crystals away from other people. The more people who touch your crystals, the more difficult it will be for the stone to zone in on your needs and wants and to build the vibrations you need to get results. If someone does touch your crystal, you'll need to cleanse it before you use it.

Chapter 4:
Chakras and Crystal Use

Before we start talking in great detail about how to use your crystals, we need to talk about chakras.

Not everyone uses crystals alongside their chakras but if you want to get the most out of crystal healing, it's best to learn about them and use them as part of your practice occasionally.

The build-up of negative energy within the body's chakras can often be the reason why good fortune isn't following and why abundance doesn't come your way. Equally, negativity can easily flow through the body as a result of a blocked chakra. Crystals can help to remedy this and allow positive energy to start flowing naturally throughout your mind, body, and spirit.

What is a Chakra?

Let's pull it right back to basics before we go on. You've no doubt heard the word 'chakra', but what does it mean exactly? Is it something you can see and feel, or is it invisible?

The word 'chakra' translates as 'wheel' in Sanskrit and it is something that is invisible to the human eye. However, those who are trained in spirituality, reiki, and other alternative medicines claim to be able to visualise the chakras and the aura surrounding the body. For you and me, however, chakras are invisible, yet extremely powerful in what they can do.

A chakra is a centre of energy. You have 7 main chakras and they spin all the time. When they don't spin or they spin slowly, that means they're blocked or struggling. The spinning energy in each chakra is associated with a specific part of the body or part of your life. To feel your very best and to have happiness and health in your life, all 7 chakras need to be working at optimum levels, balanced, and completely open.

The 7 Chakras and What They Mean

Each chakra has a colour and an associated meaning. The 7 chakras move up the body in a straight line, beginning at the bottom of the spine and ending just above the top of the head.

The 7 chakras are:

- **Root chakra** - Red in colour and located at the tailbone

- **Sacral chakra** - Orange in colour and located at the naval

- **Solar plexus chakra** - Yellow in colour and located at the centre of the chest

- **Heart chakra** - Green in colour and located where the heart is

- **Throat chakra** - Blue in colour and located at the throat

- **Third eye chakra** - Indigo in colour and located in the middle of the forehead, just above the eyes

- **Crown chakra** - Violet or white in colour and located at the top of the head

Let's take a brief look at each chakra and identify what each energy centre pertains to. Then, when using your crystals, you can meditate or even simply place the crystal on the area you need to work on.

The Root Chakra

The root chakra is located right at the bottom of the spine, where the tailbone ends. It is represented by the colour red and is associated with stability, grounding, and your general identity as an individual.

When the root chakra becomes blocked, an individual can start struggling with insecurity, often about money. Physical problems associated with a blocked root chakra include constipation, bladder issues, and arthritis.

Good crystals for unblocking the root chakra include:

- Tiger's eye
- Black tourmaline
- Obsidian
- Bloodstone
- Jasper (red)

The Sacral Chakra

The second chakra (moving up the body) is the sacral chakra, represented by the colour orange. This chakra is located just below the navel, or belly button. It is associated with creativity, sexuality, and pleasure in general. Self-worth is also an important connection with this chakra, although mostly connected to the sexual side.

When the sacral chakra is blocked or sluggish, a person may struggle with pain in the lower back, urinary tract infections, and men may also struggle with maintaining an erection.

Good crystals for unblocking the sacral chakra include:

- Citrine
- Calcite
- Orange carnelian
- Tiger's Eye

The Solar Plexus Chakra

The solar plexus chakra is represented by yellow and is located at the top of the abdomen, close to the stomach. This chakra is concerned with feelings of self-esteem and general confidence. As a result, this is a chakra that many people have problems with.

When his chakra is blocked or has any sluggish issues, digestive problems can occur, because of its close proximity to the digestive tract and stomach. You may notice heartburn, indigestion, and loss of appetite. Emotionally, a blocked chakra here may bring about feelings of low self-worth and low confidence.

Good crystals for unblocking the solar plexus chakra include:

- Tiger's Eye
- Citrine
- Agate
- Lemon quartz
- Jasper

The Heart Chakra

As the name suggests, the heart chakra is located in the middle of the chest, around the heart. It is represented by the colour green, and not pink or red as many would expect. The heart chakra is typically associated with compassion, love for others, and self-love.

When the heart chakra is experiencing problems, an individual may struggle with their body weight, experience heart issues, and breathing problems, such as asthma. It's also possible that a blocked heart chakra may cause someone to act in an unkind way, or to show a lack of love and compassion. A problem in this chakra can often cause people to put themselves last, therefore struggling with their own self-worth. This can affect how they connect to others and how they conduct their relationships. Feelings of loneliness and insecurity are also problems here.

Good crystals for unblocking the heart chakra include:

- Rose quartz
- Amethyst
- Green jade
- Rhodochrosite
- Green aventurine

The Throat Chakra

Moving up the body in a direct and straight line we have the throat chakra next. This is represented by the colour blue, and as you would expect, it is located where at the throat. This chakra is all about communication and being able to speak the truth or thinking before you speak.

When the throat chakra is blocked or out of alignment, a person may have tooth or mouth problems, including the gums. Problems can also show in a person's actions as they may speak quickly, without thinking first, gossip, or speak over other people, therefore taking over a conversation. Problems here often cause a person to be untrue to themselves and therefore bringing this chakra into check is important for a strong and fulfilling life.

Good crystals for unblocking the throat chakra include:

- Aquamarine
- Angelite
- Blue Apatite

- Blue lace agate
- Chrysocolla

The Third Eye Chakra

You might also hear this chakra referred to as the brow chakra, but it is one and the same thing. It is represented by the colour indigo, and it is located just above the eyebrows, in the middle of the forehead. This chakra is associated with imagination, creativity, and intuition.

A problem with the third eye chakra can often cause headaches and even migraines. It can also cause problems with focus, concentration, and can even cause hearing issues. If you struggle to trust your intuition and be guided by it, you may have a problem with your third eye chakra. This chakra is also associated with those who are starting to tap into their spirituality.

Good crystals for unlocking the third eye chakra include:

- Amethyst
- Sapphire

- Rhondite
- Tourmaline (purple and violet)

The Crown Chakra

The final chakra is the crown chakra. You will see this chakra either represented by violet or white and it is located at the highest point of the head. This chakra is associated with spirality, higher awareness, intelligence, and enlightenment. When this chakra is working well, you can see the bigger picture and you can connect to whatever your purpose in life is.

However, when the crown chakra is blocked or out of alignment, it affects every other chakra in the body. Therefore, it can connect any organ or system in the body too. Since the crown chakra is connected strongly with spirality and purpose, problems her can cause major issues in life. A person with a problem in this area may become closed-minded, stubborn, or very sceptical of people, untrusting even.

Good crystals for unblocking the crown chakra are:

- Amethyst
- Clear quartz
- Lepidolite
- Labradorite
- White agate
- Moonstone

How do Crystals Help The Chakras?

In our next chapter, we're going to talk in detail about how to get started with crystals and one of those methods will include meditating and also placing a specific crystal where the chakra is located on the body.

It's important to use the right type of crystal when you're trying to aim your efforts towards unblocking or alignment an out-of-whack chakra. For instance, using amethyst on your sacral chakra might do something, but it's not going to give you the benefit that the suggested crystals would.

When a chakra becomes blocked, it is blocked with negative or bad energy. The crystals and their vibrations help to loosen that energy and absorb it. The chakra is then able to spin as it is supposed to, bringing the area into harmony and balance once more. The area is cleansed of toxic and negativity and therefore revitalised.

Chapter 4:

Getting Started With Crystal Healing

Up to this point, we've talked about the basics of crystal healing and explained about the different stones, what they do, and the chakras too. Now, it's time to put all of this new knowledge into action!

In this bumper chapter, you're going to learn how to get started with crystal healing. Not only that, but you're also going to be able to start using your crystal of choice straightaway. You'll find exercises and methods to try.

Which one should you start with?

That's a personal choice! We talked earlier about allowing your intuition to guide you when finding the right crystal for your needs. The same method can be used when working out how best to use your crystal. Read this chapter thoroughly and then allow your intuition to pull you towards the method that appeals to you the most.

However, do remember that crystal healing is new to you. Don't try and run before you can walk! It might be best to start holding your crystal and becoming comfortable with it before you start meditating or trying to manifest wealth or love.

There is no right or wrong answer when it comes to speed of use. You can move through the methods in a way that suits you but do try and really give your all when using your crystal. Remember, it will give back what you give to it - if you believe in its powers and really allow it to guide you and bring benefit to your life, it will work much harder for you. However, if you allow scepticism to run amok, you're not going to find much benefit coming your way.

So, clear your mind, and let's get started!

Programming Your Crystal

You already know that when you first get your crystal, you need to cleanse it to rid it of any lingering negative energies that have been placed upon it by someone else. Once you've done that and allowed it to dry out in natural early sunlight or the light of a full moon, you then need to give it a few clues as to what you want it to do for you.

This is called programming.

Every crystal has a specific set of strengths. For instance, we've talked about the fact that rose quartz is ideal for helping with matters of romance and self-love. We know that the sapphire is a great stone for boosting wisdom. The list goes on. However, each crystal has more than one use. Your crystal is very powerful and has a lot of benefits to bring to you, but you have to tell it what you want. Without that, you may end up with something completely different!

Your crystal will start to use its natural vibrations once it has been programmed. This means that you tell it what you want, and it then receives its overall purpose. You can do this at any time, but it's ideal to program your crystal after you've cleansed it. That way, you know it's not harbouring any lingering negativity and it's clean and ready to start bringing the benefits you want.

You'll find many different methods for programming and as with anything related to crystal healing, it really comes down to finding the method that suits you best. Before you begin programming, make sure that you've spent time really thinking about what you want your crystal to do. Remember the journaling idea we spoke about earlier in the book? That's what you need to do before you start cleansing and programming your crystal.

- Take your newly cleansed crystal and hold it in your left hand

- It's a good idea to stand next to the window so the natural light can touch the crystal as you program it

- Close your eyes and take a breath, grounding yourself and connecting fully with the crystal

- Speak out loud, saying "I program this crystal to ....." And insert the purpose you want it to fulfil in the blank

- Repeat the words three times - your left-hand side is your receiving side, i.e. you're receiving whatever the crystal is going to give to you, and saying something three times represents action

- Close your eyes once more and feel the crystal in your hand. Focus on visualising the crystal absorbing the intention you've just set. If you can, try and visualise yourself receiving the intention you've asked for. So, if you asked to feel more confident, visualise how that would feel

- Give thanks to your crystal ahead of time

- It's a good idea to carry your crystal with you, on your left-hand side, to further allow it to connect with your energies.

You might sometimes hear programming referred to as 'charging' but this process is one and the same.

As you start to use your crystal, something we're going to explore more shortly, always go back to the visualisation step. A few times every day, hold the crystal in your left hand and go back to visualising yourself receiving the very thing you asked for. What does it look like? What does it feel like? Be as detailed as possible and by doing that, you're raising the vibrations within the crystal and increasing the likelihood of you getting what you're asking for.

It's normal to have doubts every now and again, especially if you're new to crystal healing. Try and push those doubts to the back of your mind because the more you allow them to interfere with your intended outcome, the less likely it is to come true. When programming your crystal, you need to believe with your entire being that it's going to happen.

So, cleansing your crystal is the first step, and programming it is the second. From there, you can opt to use a range of different methods when using your crystal in your day-to-day life, or simply ad-hoc, when you want to reconnect with your initial intention. Of course, it goes without saying that the more you use your crystal, the stronger it will become. Don't just throw it to the back of your bedroom drawers and expect it to do what you've asked it to do - you need to put in the work too!

Simply Holding Your Crystal

When programming your crystal, you held it in your left hand. There is a very good reason for that. Your left-hand side is said to be the receiving side of your body. You're keen to receive what you've asked for from your crystal. That doesn't mean that if you hold it with your right hand, it's not going to work, but you're amplifying the crystal's vibrations and your connection with it by holding it in your left hand.

When holding your crystal, hold it in the centre of your palm and close your fingers around it. Feel the weight of it in the centre of your hand and notice how it feels. Does it feel smooth? Rough? Open your hand and look at the crystal - does it glisten in the light? Is there a pattern to its markings? The more familiar you become with your crystal the more it will connect with you.

A little later we're going to talk about meditation. That is something which some people find worrying to do at the start because they assume that it means completely clearing your mind. Of course, that can be difficult with the constant noise we surround ourselves with. However, meditation can be done with your eyes open and your awareness totally in the moment. That's partly what holding your crystal is - slight meditation.

Set some time aside every single day to spend some time with your crystal. It's at this point that you can go back to the visualisation step we talked about in our last section. Make sure that you choose a time when you're not distracted or a time when you need to go somewhere relatively soon. You need to be able to settle down and focus on your crystal.

Regularly handling your crystal is important in building up a connection and really feeling those vibrations. However, you should be careful that you don't let anyone else touch your crystal. If that happens, it could absorb energies from that person, especially negative energies. That could interfere with the crystal helping you in your purpose.

Meditation With Your Crystal

Ah, meditation. The one word which makes people roll their eyes. The reason so many people are a little on the fence about mediation is that it's full of total misunderstandings.

Many people think that meditation involves chanting, going into a trance-like state, and clearing the mind completely. That's not what meditation has to be at all. For sure, you can do meditation in that way if you've practiced for a very long time, and it suits you. But you don't have to do that. Meditation is a personal deal. There is no right or wrong way to do it; simply what works for you versus what doesn't.

If you ask a group of people who meditate regularly how they go about it, you'll find a range of answers heading your way. What works for one person doesn't always work for another, but there are general guidelines you can use to help you.

Meditation is basically about turning your attention inwards. It allows you the chance to quiet your mind and cut out the chatter. Then, you can listen to any messages that are coming from your subconscious and your higher self. Crystals can help you to focus, simply by holding them in your hand. That way, you're more likely to cut out the noise and be able to get the most out of your meditation session - the aim is to listen to your inner voice because that's where the truth often lies.

The benefits of meditating with crystals include:

- Gives you something to focus on during meditating, therefore making it easier for beginners

- Allows you to focus on the outcome, with a better chance of achieving it

- Gives a greater amount of reinforcement to the thing you programmed your crystal to do, i.e., your intention

- Helps to raise personal awareness

- Allows you to focus on and trust your intuition more easily and become more insightful as a result

Let's look at a few different ways you can try crystal meditation for the first time. Some methods we've mentioned in passing already and others we're going to delve into in more detail shortly. For now, know that crystal meditation is the ideal way to connect with your crystal while also allowing you to dig deep and listen to your intuition.

Grounding Yourself

The first step is to ground yourself.

Sit down somewhere comfortable or lay down if you prefer. Make sure that you're not too hot or cold and that you're not wearing restrictive clothing that could distract your mind. Also, make sure that you choose a time of day free of distractions and don't decide to meditate half an hour before you go out! You need to be able to fully relax and you won't be able to do that if you have one eye on the clock.

It goes without saying that you turn your phone onto silent, or better still, turn it off.

- Hold your crystal in your left hand and feel the weight of it in your palm

- Bring your hands in front of you and clasp both hands, holding the crystal in both

- Close your eyes and turn your attention to your breath

- Breathe in through your nose for a slow count of five, taking your time and not rushing

- Hold your breath for two seconds

- Exhale through your mouth for another slow count of five, controlling the exhale

- Repeat this deep breathing, grounding exercise until you feel like your mind is starting to quieten. This may take up to 10 or more breaths, depending on how easy you find it to turn your attention fully inwards

- Now, turn your attention to the crystal in your hand. Really focus your mind on it and visualise it in your mind

- Can you feel anything in your hand other than its weight? Some crystals resonate, i.e. they vibrate subtly in the palm of your hand, especially if they're programmed and really connected to you. You might not feel a buzzing per se, but you may feel a sensation somewhere. It may not be your hands, it may be a tingling on the back of your neck, or perhaps a gentle buzzing sensation in general. Scan your body at this point and look for any resonating signs. However, do be aware that not all crystals do this, so don't panic if you don't feel anything; it's simply a way to connect you to your crystal meditation session

- If at any time you feel your thoughts wandering, go back to the initial breathing exercise to ground you once more.

This exercise grounds you so you can start to meditate with a clear mind. Some people find it useful to visualise a protective white light around them as they're meditating. It helps them to feel safer, but it's not something you absolutely have to do.

Crystal Exploration Meditation

Let's look at another crystal meditation exercise you can try. This particular meditation will help you fully connect with your crystal, therefore amplifying the vibrations and their connection to you and your initial purpose.

Again, make sure you have cleansed and programmed your crystal and that you've carried it around with you for a few days at least. Perform the grounding exercise we've just talked about before you start this exercise, to clear your mind completely.

When you're ready, try this:

- As you hold the crystal in both hands before you (with your eyes closed), turn your attention to the feeling of it in your hands once more. When you're ready, try to pull your mind closer to the crystal, visualising it in your mind, getting closer and closer to it, until you're almost a miniature version of yourself and the crystal stands towering over you, inviting you to enter inside

- Visualise yourself touching the crystal's walls. Feel whether they're smooth or rough. Are there any sharp parts? Be as detailed as you can possibly be

- Now, visualise a door on the crystal walls. Open the door and walk inside. Feel the door close behind you, causing an echo as you enter the crystal's interior

- What do you see? Explore the feel of the walls. Touch them and feel whether they're warm, cold, smooth, or rough. What is the light like around you? Can you hear anything? Be as detailed as possible once more and really take the time to get inside the crystal and familiarise yourself with it

- When you're ready, start to dig deeper. What can you feel when you're inside the crystal? Can you feel a gentle humming vibration? Does it feel warm or is the temperature low?

- When you've explored the inside of your crystal as much as you can, spending at least a few minutes losing yourself in the meditation, tell yourself that you're going to exit the crystal

- Slowly make your way towards the door, exactly in the same spot where you walked in. Turn around to look at the interior of your crystal once more and thank it for hosting you during your exploration

- When you're ready, walk out of the door and close it behind you. Slowly visualise walking away from the crystal so it becomes smaller and smaller and you grow in height until you're back to your regular size
- Slowly open your eyes and sit quietly for a short while, feeling the crystal still in your hands.

Listening to Messages From Your Crystal

The first meditation exercise we talked about helped you to ground yourself during meditation and connect with your crystal. This particular exercise will help you to tune into any messages your crystal wants to send you. It's important to be patient with this type of meditation and don't jump straight into it the moment you program your crystal.

Give yourself some time and connect with your crystal over a few days or weeks. After you've visualised your intention several times, try this particular exercise.

Of course, ground yourself before you start your meditation, going back to our first exercise.

- Spend around 3 minutes focusing on your breath to get rid of any chatter inside your brain. If you notice that your thoughts start to edge back in, turn your attention back to your breath once more to pull your mind back to the centre

- Take the crystal and hold it in your hands

- Ask the crystal for permission to meditate with it and seek any guidance or messages it wants to give you

- Hold the crystal in your left hand, in a way that feels easy to you

- Can you feel anything within your body? This is likely to be how your crystal wants to connect with you and communicate. It might be that you see colours behind your closed eyelids, you might feel a warmth in your hand or throughout your body, or you might even see images appearing in your mind. Spend some time looking for signs and remember to be patient. It might not come to you straightaway, or at least the first few times you try this meditation exercise

- Be open to any messages that come to you. These may not be in verbal form. You might notice odd keywords appearing in your mind, maybe you'll hear a voice or your own voice. You might see pictures that give you a message that way. Explore these and remember them. You need to scribble these down once you've finished your meditation

- Once you think you've gained everything you can for this session, thank the crystal for its help and turn your attention back to your breath for a few minutes

- When you're ready, open your eyes and grab a notebook, scribbling down whatever you found from your mediation session

Keep a record of your findings from your crystal meditation sessions. It's a good idea to jot these down in a meditation diary. It could be that your crystal gives you a series of messages that don't mean anything to begin with, but over time they start to build a picture. Give it a week or two of meditating and then take a look over your journal entries and look for patterns or a connection between the messages.

Getting What You Want Meditation

Earlier in this chapter, we talked about programming your crystal. Part of that was visualizing what you wanted the crystal to do, i.e., your intention. We asked you to focus on what it would feel like when you are granted what you asked for. However, it could be that what you ask for isn't what you want after all.

It's important to be open to the possibility that the thing you want may not be good for you. Or it might be that you can have what you want and it will be perfectly good, but that you need to be wary of something to avoid it taking a negative route. For instance, you may wish for wealth but too much money may make you wasteful. Your crystals may want to teach you that lesson before you are given what you want.

This particular meditation helps you to zone in on any particular warnings or lessons but it's also a good exercise for helping you to tune in to your intuition.

- As before, ground yourself and hold your crystal in your hand

- Start to visualise what you've asked your crystal to do, i.e. your intention

- Add as much detail as you can. Explore what it looks like, feels like, etc

- However, also pay a lot of attention to how you feel as you're visualising. Can you feel anything in your gut? Do you feel happy as you're visualising and comfortable? Or, do you feel a little wary or uncomfortable at all? You don't need to explore comfortable feelings any further, but anything that makes you feel slightly 'off' needs to be focused on and explored a little further

- If you do feel wary or uncomfortable of anything, zone in on that feeling and try to ask for answers from your crystal. Listen to any messages that come from the crystal, as per our last exercise

- Once you've finished, thank your crystal for its guidance and focus on your breath for a while before opening your eyes

- Write down anything you gained from your meditation and try to piece together messages.

Sometimes we think we know what we want. However, what we want isn't always what is best for us. Your higher self and your intuition already know this, but the rest of you is yet to catch up. Your crystal connects you to that higher self and therefore allows messages to flow down to you.

These are a few crystals meditation exercises you can try for yourself. They're also ideal for beginners. However, remember to give it time and don't give up if you don't get the information, you want immediately.

Those who regularly meditate and find it easy to quieten their mind have practiced many times over the years. This type of skill doesn't happen overnight. The more you practice, the easier it will become. Also, your crystal may not give you the answers or connection you want straightaway. Be patient!

Balancing And Unblocking Chakras with Crystals

Now you're a little more familiar with crystal meditation as a whole, you can take things a step further and work with your chakras.

In our previous chapter, we talked about the different chakras and what they represent. You can use that information to work out whether you indeed may have a problem with a specific chakra that needs unblocking or aligning once more. Chakras are meant to spin and if one of your chakras isn't spinning or isn't spinning as quickly as the others, you need to address it. Doing that will help you to avoid physical and emotional symptoms.

It's also worth noting that one blocked or problematic chakra can cause the others to be out of whack too. You may feel generally sluggish or unwell. You might notice that your immune system isn't functioning well and you're catching every virus and bug flying around.

Realigning and ensuring the free flow of energy through your chakras is vital to a healthy and happy life.

There are two ways you can approach using crystals to help with problematic chakras. The first is to identify the problematic chakra and work with it individually. The second is to do a full body grid and work through each chakra.

Addressing a Particular Chakra With Crystals

If you know which chakra you need to work on, choose the right crystal for the job. For instance, if you have problematic heart chakra, you may choose rose quartz. If you think your third eye chakra needs some work, amethyst is a good choice. You can refer back to our chapter on chakras if you need a reminder of the particular crystals that help with specific chakras.

- Lay down and make yourself comfortable. Close the curtains or simply create an environment that is serene and peaceful

- Close your eyes and focus on your breath in the same way you would if you were meditating

- When you're ready, take the crystal and place it on your body, where the corresponding chakra is located

- Close your eyes once more and turn your attention to where the crystal is located

- Remember to breathe in a slow and steady manner

- For this type of meditation, you don't need to visualise anything in particular, although if you want to focus on the chakra opening, you can do so. Otherwise, simply keep your focus on your breath and allow the crystal to do its work.

This type of exercise will help to create a swirl of positive energy around the chakra that is causing you the problem. The crystal will absorb the negative energy that may be blocking the chakra and help it to start spinning in alignment once more. You may need to do this several times before you notice a difference but be sure to give it a little time before ending your meditation session. How long you lay there for is up to you, but it needs to be more than a few minutes to gain major benefit!

You may also notice that as you unblock a particular chakra, you notice emotional situations arising. This is because the chakra was blocked due to a problem that you now need to address. For instance, you may have problems with your heart chakra because you have a habit of holding on to resentment from previous relationships. Unblocking that chakra will allow the energy to flow, but you need to address that issue in order to ensure it doesn't block itself again. Your crystal will help you to understand what needs to be done by asking for messages during meditation sessions, such as the one we talked about in our last section.

You don't necessarily need a blocked or problematic chakra to start using crystals with your chakras in this way. For instance, you could use rose quartz over your heart chakra to make you more open to a new relationship. You could perhaps use a crystal over your crown chakra, such as clear quartz, to seek guidance with a specific problem, while visualising that problem at the same time. If you're struggling with meditation and you're lacking in patience, use a crystal with your third eye chakra to help the process along a little.

You don't necessarily need to be struggling with a chakra problem to use crystals in this way. You simply need to know what each chakra is responsible for and the crystals that work well with them. Then, you can try to gain benefits by using both at the same time.

Using a Full Body Grid

A full body grid helps you to bring all of your chakras into alignment. This can be a useful exercise to do every so often, perhaps once or twice a month, to ensure that all of your chakras are working well and not adversely affecting each other.

Before you start, you need to create your grid. Either draw a picture of the chakras and their associated colours, working from the root chakra up to the crown chakra, or print one out from online resources. Once you have the chakras, you need to align a crystal with each one. Again, it needs to be a crystal that works well with that particular chakra, as we talked about in our earlier chapter.

Identify your crystals and line them up with your chakras on the sheet. Once you have that, you're ready to start.

- Lay down and make yourself comfortable, ensuring that the environment is quiet and calm
- Take one crystal at a time and place it on the corresponding chakra, making sure that you're correct with where you're placing it
- Close your eyes and focus on your breathing. Stick with the exercise for half an hour at least, so make sure you have time and you're not going to be disturbed

- Start with the root chakra at the tailbone and focus on it. Visualise the crystal's vibrations absorbing into the chakra. Picture it cleaning it out thoroughly and allowing it to unblock and start spinning again

- Move up through the chakras, ending your full body grid exercise with the crown chakra at the top of the head

- Lay comfortable for a few minutes afterwards, focusing on your breath and noticing how you feel within yourself.

Crystals and chakras work together really well and help you to focus on something as you're meditating. The crystal is also perfect for absorbing negativity and helping to cleanse the chakra.

Of course, once you've finished using crystals in this manner, you'll need to cleanse them to rid them of any negative energy it has absorbed from your blocked or problematic chakra. You would do that in exactly the same way we talked about at the start of this chapter.

Then, if you want to program your crystal again, you can do so.

Creating a Crystal Grid

If you want to manifest something into your life, be it love, confidence, wealth, etc., a crystal grid could help you achieve your aim. This is a group of different crystals which are arranged into a grid pattern. The purpose is to add strength to the work the crystals are doing, magnifying their vibrations, and therefore giving them a boost of extra power.

Your crystals need to be chosen carefully. You need to know that the crystals you've chosen are all associated with the type of intention you want to manifest. Then, you need to arrange them in the specified geometric pattern. This pattern is ancient and has been used for centuries in manifestation and healing practices. There is nothing otherworldly or worrisome about this, it simply gives your crystals more power than they would otherwise have.

Let's look at a step-by-step guide on how to create your crystal grid and start using it.

Be Mindful of Your Intention

Before you start putting your crystal grid together, you need to know what you want. What is your intention? Do you want to attract love into your life? Do you want a new job? Are you looking for abundance in terms of money?

As with any type of crystal healing exercise, you have to be clear about what you want. You can either write it down and have it located in the middle of your crystal grid for references, or you can keep it in your mind. Either way will work just fine. All you need to do is be sure of what you're asking for.

Identify The Right Crystals

Next, you need to get your crystals together. The crystals you choose all need to be specific to your particular intention. If you're looking for money, you need to choose crystals that are associated with wealth and abundance. If you're looking for love, you need to choose crystals associated with love and romance.

You also need to choose a master crystal. This should be a crystal that is most strongly associated with the thing you're trying to manifest. It should also be chosen by you and, preferably, you should have felt strongly drawn to it when you picked it. The master crystal will be placed in the centre of your grid.

Identify The Grid Pattern

Crystal grids are based on geometry, and you'll find several different arrangements out there. You simply need to take the time to do some research into them and look at them carefully. Which one calls out to you more than any other?

You can look at them on a page or on a screen and concentrate for a while. When you feel a pull towards a particular one, that's the grid you need to go with. Remember, these are sacred arrangements, and the number of crystals you need for each one varies according to the grid you choose.

Lay Down Your Crystals

Following the shape of the grid, arrange your crystals accordingly. Start from the outside and work your way in, placing a crystal where indicated. Your final crystal should be the master crystal, placed in the centre of the grid. As you lay your crystals down, make sure that you keep your initial intention in mind and purposefully place the crystals in their associated place.

Don't just put them down willy-nilly and move on to the next one - you need to do this carefully and with purpose.

Once your crystals are all down, take a clear quartz and slowly run it over the top of all the crystals, following the shape of the grid. This works to bind the crystals together and connect them to one another. By doing that, the crystals will all be working in the same direction, for the same purpose.

Activate Your Crystal Grid

You created your crystal grid with your intention in mind but now you need to activate it to ensure that all crystals are working in synergy. Thankfully, this is very easily done, much easier than it sounds!

When all your stones are laid down, take a deep breath (close your eyes if you want to, or focus on the crystals in the pattern before you) and say, "I have created this crystal grid to manifest/create ...... (speak your intention)" If you want to say why, then you can also do that. For instance, "I have created this crystal grid to manifest more confidence in my life. I want to be more comfortable in social situations".

Leave your grid in place and regularly visit it. You can meditate next to the grid, or you can simply spend time sitting and connecting with the crystals from time to time. However, don't just create your grid and then leave it there, looking pretty and not doing anything with it. The crystals and their energies are amplified by using a grid, but you need to connect yourself to it by being around it and zoning in on any messages the crystals are trying to send to you.

Using a Crystal Altar For Manifestation

A crystal grid is a good way to amplify the power of your crystals, but you can also use a crystal altar if you prefer. This is a space you visit regularly to focus, give thanks, and to manifest the things you want in your life. Your altar contains items that are significant to you and symbolic. The altar can be anything from a table to a corner desk the choice is yours.

Your altar is somewhere you can go whenever you want to find clarity or seek answers. It's also a space for appreciation, careful thinking, yoga, and meditation. This is your special space to spend time and go within, perhaps to find answers or simply to ground yourself during stressful and busy times.

Adding crystals to your altar or making an altar completely out of crystals can help you to manifest the things you want in your life. Be sure to choose crystals that are connected with your intention and program them with that very intention in mind. It's good practice to place a large standing crystal with a pointed edge in the middle as this will help to bring the crystals together and amplify their vibrations.

You can speak your intention aloud, or you can write it down on a piece of paper and place the paper underneath your pointed edge crystal.

There isn't a huge amount of technicality involved in creating a crystal altar as it's simply whatever feels right for you. However, when you're putting your altar together, be sure to think about your intention as you're doing so. That way, you're allowing the energies to start building from the get-go. You can then visit this space regularly, either to meditate or simply to focus and think about a specific subject. You can even head there to relax!

Crystals And Yoga

We all know that yoga is a beneficial practice for the mind, body, and soul. It's also fantastic exercise. Whether you're new to yoga, you've never tried it before, or you're someone who practices occasionally, you can add crystals into your yoga routine and grab some extra benefits at the same time.

There are a couple of ways you can incorporate crystals into your yoga practice.

Place Crystals Upon Your Yoga Mat

When you have cleansed and programmed your crystal, or crystals, you can simply place them down on your yoga mat and have them close to you as you're working through the poses. Of course, yoga focuses upon the breath, but it also connects with your inner self. Having your crystal close by will allow you to further deepen your intuition and you may find that as you move through the poses, you start to receive messages from your crystals.

In some ways, yoga is akin to meditation. It's no surprise that when your attention is turned inward, you're more open to receiving such messages and amplifying energy to help manifest whatever your intention is.

You can also place your crystals around you in a crystal grid as you're doing your yoga. As you move through the poses, visualise an energy grid all around you, giving you extra energy and allowing you to take your poses deeper and further.

Place Crystals on Your Body

When you're in savasana, or corpse pose, at the end of your yoga session, you can place crystals on your body. This helps to unblock any chakras with problems but can also help to boost the free flow of positive energy throughout your very being too.

To help you to drift deeper into the meditative state that savasana encourages, you can place a crystal on your third eye chakra. This will allow you to focus and may also help you to listen closely to any messages arising from your higher self and intuition.

It's possible that you will feel the slight vibrations moving through your body as you do this. That's because you're already connected to your higher self through your yoga practice and you're more open to feeling the vibrations as a result. For that reason, crystals and yoga go together perfectly.

If you've never tried yoga, it's a great addition to your crystal healing world. Yoga has a wealth of benefits, including:

- Improving balance, flexibility, and strength
- Helps with some chronic pain conditions
- May alleviate arthritis symptoms
- Helps you to relax more deeply
- Encourages a better night's sleep
- Promotes positive heart health

- Helps you to manage stress and anxiety in a more positive way
- Boosts mood
- Increases energy levels
- Gives you a gentle but steady workout

By adding crystals to your yoga sessions, you can work to boost your manifestation efforts while also allowing you a great opportunity to connect with your higher self.

Using Crystals in Your Daily Life

The exercises we've talked about so far will help you to get started with crystal healing and start manifesting all the things you want and need in life. However, you don't need to go through specific meditations or rituals to grab the benefits all the time. There are many ways you can incorporate crystals into your daily life and keep yourself connected to your precious stones.

Of course, you should always keep your original intention in mind and make sure that you think of it regularly. Continue to touch your stones and hold them regularly to align them with your intention and keep them connected to you.

Here are a few ways you can incorporate crystals into your daily life.

- **Carry your crystals daily** - Buy a soft pouch and keep your crystals in your left side pocket as you go about your daily business. As before, touch them regularly and think of your intention as you do so. This is a very simple and non-time consuming way to use crystal healing in your daily life.

- **Purchase genuine crystal jewellery** - As long as you make sure that the jewellery you're purchasing contains a genuine gemstone, there's no reason why you can't use it in exactly the same way as any other stone. Many people find jewellery a good way to use crystal healing in their daily lives. Wearing a bracelet made of genuine rose quartz on your left wrist could help to bring an abundance of self-love and respect into your life. Wearing a sapphire ring on your left hand could help you to focus, gain clarity of thought, and also connect to your intuition. Simply remember to clean your jewellery regularly and to use the same cleansing method as you would with a regular crystal.

- **Crystal home decor** - Such is the popularity of crystal healing these days that you'll find many home decor items that contain gemstones. Again, make sure that what you're purchasing contains a genuine gemstone and not a fake version. Cleanse it in the same way and state your intention, touching it regularly. It's also a good idea to place such decor items somewhere personal to you, such as your bedroom.

- **A crystal bath** - Crystals and self-care go together like salt and pepper! Run a warm bath (not too hot) and place your crystals inside the water. Bathe in the water and remember to wash your face with the water too. Simply make sure that your crystals are clean before you do so, from a hygiene point of view. This type of self-care ritual helps to cleanse you of negativity and refresh you physically, mentally, and emotionally.

- **Crystal face masks** - If you Google 'crystal face masks' you'll find a range of makes that have crystals infused into them, however, a much easier method is to use your own crystals alongside a regular sheet mask. Simply lay your sheet mask on your face and relax. Then, place your crystals at specific points on your face too. Lay back and relax for half an hour! You could use rose quartz for beauty, aquamarine for anti-aging, clear quartz for skin detoxification, or tourmaline quartz for breaking up any facial tension you may be holding without realising it.

These are easy and luxurious ways you can connect with your crystals every day. They're all accessible to everyone, you simply need to be sure that if you do purchase crystal items, such as jewellery or home goods, that you're getting exactly what you think you are. There are many fake crystals out there and you need the genuine article to benefit from its healing vibrations and energy absorption.

Home And Work Space Placement

Aside from things you can do on the daily in association with crystal healing, there are also a few things you can do in terms of space placement. Placing crystals around your home or even your work environment could help to usher in positive energy and rid the space of negative vibes.

Here are just a few simple ways you can place crystals around your home or work environment, without them becoming too much, or in the way.

- **Use a crystal grid** - A little earlier we talked about using a crystal grid to amplify the power of a group of crystals, all working in synergy towards a common aim. You can easily leave your crystal grid in a specific place in the house and connect with it on a daily basis. Simply choose a space where your grid isn't going to be disturbed or knocked over. If you have children or pets in the house, be sure to place your grid out of reach. Your grid will bring a generally positive vibe to your house and soak up any negative energy before it causes problems between you and your family members.

- **Use a crystal altar** - Again, we have talked about how you can use a crystal altar for your intentions but you can also create one in your house for decoration and purpose. Your altar needs to be somewhere you can go for peace and serenity so make sure that it's not a spot where anyone is going to interrupt you or go without your knowledge. If someone else uses your altar, it's going to soak up their energies and cause problems when you want to manifest something. Aside from that, a crystal altar can bring good fortune and positive vibes into your house.

- **Purchase crystal home decor** - Crystal decorated wind chimes, large crystals for decoration, crystal wall hangings, the list goes on. As we mentioned earlier, simply be sure that it's a genuine gemstone contained within the decor. It may cost you a little more but you know that you're getting benefits. Also, be sure to clean your decor items regularly. You can also place small decorative items in your workspace.

- **Use crystal clusters in small rooms** - You may not have space for an altar or a grid if you have a small house and in that case, you can create a mini crystal altar by simply grouping together small clusters of crystals. These can be small in size and simply arranged in a circle or a small bundle. As long as they're regularly cleaned, you handle them regularly, and you think of your intention every time you walk past them, they'll work in the same way. Small clusters are also ideal for workspaces. If you have your own desk in a large office, you could have a small cluster of crystals next to your computer. This is ideal for boosting concentration, focus, and creative thinking.

- **Decorate with large standing crystals** - We've all see the large and very heavy standing crystals that have a point on the top. They vary in size and they come in different crystal types. These are literal crystals, it's just that they've been made to be more decorative. If you don't want to use an altar but you want to have a spot where you can place your intention on a written note and leave it underneath, one of these crystals is ideal. They're also very luxurious in appearance and will probably gain admiring glances from your neighbours!

As you can see, it's easy to decorate your home and workspace with crystals. You can make it as subtle or obvious as you like and the results will remain the same, as long as your crystals are clean, programmed, and not touched by anyone else. You could even place a crystal in your car, for protection. There really is no end to the wonder of crystal healing!

Conclusion

AND THERE WE HAVE IT, everything you need to know to get started with crystal healing.

As a beginner, it's normal to look at a subject such as this and be confused or overwhelmed. The good news is that crystal healing isn't actually that complicated. All you need to do is believe in it. For sure, that's easier said than done if you are a sceptic where anything new age or alternative is concerned. Yet, crystals have been used in healing for many centuries and when something has hung around for that long, surely there has to be some truth in it?

Whether scientists believe in the healing power of precious gemstones or not, doesn't matter. What matters is what you believe. If you truly believe that your crystal is going to bring you the very thing you've programmed it for, it will do so. Your mind needs to be open to receiving for this type of alternative therapy to work. You're not alone either, millions of people regularly use crystals for a variety of different means.

Your first step is to know what you want or need. From there, you simply need to open your mind and find the crystal that is going to help you tick that box.

From time to time we all need a little extra boost in a particular part of our lives. It could be that you've been through a tough breakup, and it's left you feeling lacking in self-worth and confidence. Maybe you've been stuck in the same job for years and you feel like you're not able to do anything else. Perhaps you're struggling with the loss of a loved one and the dark cloud over your head doesn't seem to be passing.

Reaching out to an alternative therapy could be what you need to help bring positive energy into your life. Once you start to focus on the positives and stop being so drenched in negativity, you will notice a wealth of opportunities all around you.

The great thing about crystal healing is that it's not hard to do. For sure, meditation takes time and effort to master, but it's something that anyone can begin with. You don't have to be able to do a particular thing or have any qualifications to try meditation. It's simply that you need to give it time and persevere. With patience, you'll be able to see an improvement in your concentration levels over time. You may never be a meditation master and be able to zone out for hours at a time, but that's not what you're aiming to do. You're aiming to encourage positivity into your life and manifest a specific intention.

All that's left to do is to get started. You will never know if crystals are for you unless you try. These beautiful, precious, and ancient gemstones hold more power than we will ever know, and they can help you to become healthier, happier, more aware, and wealthier too. For those countless who have picked up a crystal, tried it for a few days, and given up because they didn't see a major change in their life, crystals didn't work. Do you know why? Because they weren't serious about using crystals for healing and they didn't give it enough time.

You're not going to make that mistake because you've read this book. You know that you need to be patient. You know that you need to choose your crystals carefully and pay them respect. You know that you need to cleanse and program your crystals and that nobody else should touch them. You also know how to use them to the best of their ability. You're aware of meditation, you know that you need to practice and give it time. You know that the more you practice, the better at it you'll become.

You also know how to amplify the power of the crystals and use them in your daily life. You literally have everything you could possibly need within you already.

This book will be there for you if you have any queries or questions. Simply go back to the relevant section and re-read it once more. There is a lot of information contained within these pages and nobody expects you to remember it all at once!

Consider this book your guide. It will hold your hand through your new journey, and it will give you the confidence you need to keep going when you're not sure if it's working. Because the truth is, crystals will make you wait a while. They'll test you to make sure that you really do want what you've asked for. But, if you show them, you're serious and if you're patient, the one thing you've asked for can be yours.

So, what do you want? Give it some serious thought and be firm in your mind. Once you've done that, the only way is up. The crystals are waiting to give you everything you want and desire. You just need to know the right way to use them.

Disclaimer

This book contains opinions and ideas of the author and is meant to teach the reader informative and helpful knowledge while due care should be taken by the user in the application of the information provided. The instructions and strategies are possibly not right for every reader and there is no guarantee that they work for everyone. Using this book and implementing the information/recipes therein contained is explicitly your own responsibility and risk. This work with all its contents does not guarantee correctness, completion, quality, or correctness of the provided information. Misinformation or misprints cannot be completely eliminated.

Printed in Great Britain
by Amazon